A DICKENS
OF A CAROL

A DICKENS OF A CAROL

Kimberley Lynne

Baltimore, Maryland
www.apprenticehouse.com

© 2010, Kimberley Lynne

Library of Congress Cataloging-in-Publication Data

Lynne, Kimberley, 1961-
A Dickens of a Carol / Kimberley Lynne.
p. cm.
ISBN 978-1-934074-14-5
1. Dickens, Charles, 1812-1870–Drama. 2. Christmas plays.
I. Title.
PS3612.Y552D53 2008
812'.6–dc22
2007051088

All rights reserved. No part of this book may be reproduced or transmitted in any form or by any means, electronic or mechanical, including photocopy, recording, or any information storage and retrieval system, without prior permission from the publisher (except by reviewers who may quote brief passages).

Printed in the United States of America

First Edition

Published by Apprentice House
The Future of Publishing...Today!

Apprentice House
Communication Department
Loyola Univeristy Maryland
4501 N. Charles Street
Baltimore, MD 21210

410.617.5265
www.ApprenticeHouse.com • info@ApprenticeHouse.com

Dedicated to James Kinstle

FIRST PERFORMED

A Dickens of a Carol was first performed at Baltimore Shakespeare Festival in December 2003 and subsequently in December 2004 with the following cast:

Charles Dickens	James Kinstle
Director	Kathy Feininger
Scenic Design	Robert Marietta
Lighting Design	Todd Mion
Costume Design	William E. Crowther
Organist/composer	Simon Zaleski
Stage Manager	Shawn Dean

TABLE OF CONTENTS

FOREWORD XI

INTRODUCTION............................ XIII

ACT ONE, SCENE ONE 1
Stave One: Marley's Ghost

ACT ONE, SCENE TWO 18
Stave Two: The First of Three Spirits

ACT TWO, SCENE ONE 29
Stave Three: The Second of Three Spirits
Stave Four: The Last of the Spirits

ACT TWO, SCENE TWO.............................. 44
Stave Five: The End of It

ENDNOTES 55

FOREWORD

In the spring of 2003, the Artistic Director of The Baltimore Shakespeare Festival asked if I would be interested in directing their holiday show. He informed me that the show was commissioned from their "living" resident playwright and he excitedly explained that it was a one-man show chronicling Charles Dickens's process and experiences while writing *A Christmas Carol*. The "one man" in this case would be the Artistic Director himself, and during the course of the show he would play all twenty-two roles including the characters from Dickens's famous tome, Dickens himself, and several people from Dickens's life. He ended by adding that the playwright would be in residence.

I was intrigued.

I had a great deal of experience with Dickens in general and *A Christmas Carol* in particular. I also had experience working with the Artistic Director, having previously directed him in several productions. I had met the playwright, Kimberley Lynne, but never worked with her. The proposition sounded like one of those situations that would either go horribly well or horribly awry.

I am happy to say that I accepted the position and delighted to say that the resulting show turned out horribly well.

The idea behind *A Dickens of a Carol* was fascinating.

Ms. Lynne had taken Dickens's own writings about his experiences and influences while writing *A Christmas Carol* and interwoven them with the "Christmas Carol" text. The resulting script was a lively illustration of Dickens's process of discovery and creation. It was a new take on an old classic--it was an expose–exposing the tortured process of Dickens and illustrating how real life events influenced his writing.

The difficulty for playwright and director became how to breathe life into what was essentially a play composed of nothing but quotations. As we began work, I soon learned that Ms. Lynne was not only extremely knowledgeable about the life and times of Charles Dickens, but she was also as capable a storyteller as her subject. She was able to order the quotations from Dickens's letters (and those of his wife) into the perfect framework on which to hang the story of *A Christmas Carol*. As we struggled with how much information was relevant to the dramatic action and how much was holding the story back, how to structure transitions between characters all being played by one actor and how to let go of our various favorite bits that did not advance the story, I learned that Ms. Lynne was also a solid dramatist. The resulting piece is a wonderful vehicle for a talented actor and a formidable challenge for actor and director. *A Dickens of a Carol* is an innovative dramatic vebicle that illustrates for an audience the tortured genius of Charles Dickens and the striking similarities between Dickens's characters and the people and situations in his real life. The script also offers theatre practitioners a chance to communicate a fresh version of one of the greatest Christmas stories ever told.

Collaborating with Kimberley Lynne on the original production of *A Dickens of a Carol* is one of those perfect experiences that come along so seldom in an artist's career. I hope you enjoy *A Dickens of a Carol* as much as I did and continue to do. It is as fascinating to me upon the umpteenth reading as it was on the first.

Kathy Feininger
Director, Baltimore Shakespeare Festival's *A Dickens of a Carol*
Chief Creative Officer of Chanticleer Productions

INTRODUCTION

By Norrie Epstein, Author of The Friendly Dickens

Kimberley Lynne's *Dickens of a Carol* opens with a single anguished cry of "Mary!" Not Marley, but Mary. And the line is uttered by Dickens, who is the central—indeed, the only—character in the play.

Dickens would have appreciated this opening stunner.

After all, *A Christmas Carol* was designed to jolt his readers out of their smugness. Lynne's *Carol* is different, but no less Dickensian.

It is October, 1843. Dickens has frantically barricaded himself in his study to avoid domestic interruptions. During his self-imposed imprisonment, he fiddles with objects; he writes to his good friend Forester, all the while his mind wandering back to a figure that haunts him more than any other: Mary Hogarth.

Seven years before, Dickens, his bride Catherine, and her sister Mary, were returning from a night at the theatre, when suddenly Mary collapsed into a coma from which she would never recover.

In this is one-man show, "Mary" doesn't appear as a separate character, but as a projection of Dickens's fevered imagination. Costumed in a black cloak, the dead girl is reanimated, speaking through the character of Dickens.

In the end, Dickens conjures the memories, exorcizes them, and moves on, just as Scrooge is finally liberated by "ghostly visitations."

ACT ONE, SCENE ONE
Stave One: Marley's Ghost

Charles Dickens is asleep in his armchair in his study in No. 1 Devonshire Terrace, Regent's Park in London. Dickens snored. He wore perfume and carried a coin purse. He's wearing his deceased sister-in-law Mary's signet ring (gold with a white stone) on his left hand. A side table holds a candle, a green cup full of fresh flowers, a china monkey and a bell. A lap writing desk and a trunk full of Mary's clothes sit beside him. Papers and books are scattered. Hand or tabletop mirror is somewhere. Dickens drinks brandy throughout the action. Through his discovery of the story, he acts out the characters, jots down notes in shorthand, refers to existing notes, spouts the narrative verbatim and writes chunks. It is October of 1843. Dickens is 31 years old.

The actor performs all the lines. It is not necessary for the actor to say the Christmas Carol narrative in parenthetical. It can be the director's choice to amplify the actor on some of the ghost lines. He can dress in Mary's old clothes when he portrays female characters. An organist who wrote original themes for each of the ghosts accompanied the original BSF production.

Charles:
MARY! Don't go inside, Mary! Don't leave me!

(Dickens sits bolt upright from sleep.)

"Marley was dead: to begin with. There was no doubt whatever about that. The register of his burial was signed by the clergyman, the clerk, the undertaker, and the chief mourner. Scrooge signed it . . . Old Marley was dead as a door-nail."[1]

A ghost story, it's a ghost story, not a depressing pamphlet on the miserable conditions of the overcrowded workhouses! A Christmas ghost story!

Charles as Marley:
(Amplified.)

Ebenezer Scrooge!

Charles:
"Marley's voice, no doubt about it." [2]

(He listens for more. Nothing. He takes notes.)

"Scrooge knew he was dead? Of course he did. How could it be otherwise? Scrooge and he were partners for I don't know how many years... There is no doubt that Marley was dead. This must be distinctly understood, or nothing wonderful can come of the story I am going to relate." [3]

(Searches wildly through the papers in folios in the trunk. As he searches.)

"If we were not perfectly convinced that Hamlet's Father died before the play began, there would be nothing ... remarkable in his taking a stroll at night ... upon his own ramparts ... literally to astonish his son's weak mind." [4]

Damnation! Where is it? Something about an old man, something she said at Forster's last month, something about a vile old man creeping along Marylebone Road in a thick fog, clutching a lockbox.

(Finds his note and reads.)

As I came around a corner, he nearly ran into me.

He was wearing a coat as old as I am, and his face was hard and sharp as flint. Although it was only early September, the cold within him froze his own nose.

(Writes <u>Carol.</u>)

"Oh! But he was a tight-fisted hand at the grindstone, Scrooge, a squeezing, wrenching, grasping, scraping, clutching, covetous old sinner! Hard and sharp as flint . . . secret, and self-contained, and solitary as an oyster. The cold within him froze his old features, nipped his pointed nose, shriveled his cheek, stiffened his gait; made his eyes red, his thin lips blue; and spoke out shrewdly in his grating voice . . . He carried his own low temperature always about with him; he iced his office in the dog-days; and didn't thaw it one degree at Christmas." [5]

Dog-days!

(He laughs at his own work.)

Like the seemingly endless dog-days in the dull office of Ellis & Blackwell when I was fifteen. I fought so hard to climb out of the Southwark sewer, and that clerk position was the first step of my journey.

(Picks up paper he's just written.)

Where is this taking me, this story? Where are you leading me, Mary?

(Pulls out a fresh page of parchment and begins writing a letter.)

Dear Forster, woke from the middle of a tormented dream about Mary; dear, lost, gentle

Mary. I followed her through foggy city streets, and she led me to a dingy office and so the story began. Now, the room's cold, and Catherine's missing. "The presence of my wife aggravates me. I loathe my parents ... I begin to have thoughts ... of the razor upstairs, of the chemists down the street ... of hanging myself upon the pear-tree in the garden, of abstaining from food and starving myself to death." [6] "So, do you come, and sit here, and read, or work, or do something, while I write." [7] What I wouldn't give to split a bottle with you.

As Catherine:
(Sound of a door opening and Catherine stumbling in. Morning sounds underneath, including children playing.)

Oh, my gracious, oh! Mr. Dickens? Good morning, Mr. Dickens.

Charles:
(Looking up from his writing.)

Is it morning? "Why don't you ... be more careful, Mouse?" [8]

As Catherine:
I am careful, but I am such a stumbler. I do concentrate when I walk.

Charles:
I'm writing something short for the Christmas season, not in installments, but all at once. Have the servants give me wide berth. All food delivery and cleaning by you or the elder children, please.

As Catherine:
But you're still working on <u>Martin Chezzlwit</u> ...

Charles:
I like the overlap; is it cold in here to you?

As Catherine:
(Sound of the tray clumsily set down.)

It's always cold in here to me. I'll send Charley with more coal. The wallpapering workmen arrive this morning, so I'll keep the children . . .

Charles:
Wallpapering's a messy business; they must hang drop cloths! Dust kills! Mind the dust! Dust and dirt might have taxed our Mary's tired heart, God rest her soul!

(Continues writing the letter.)

Forster, how Catherine the Mouse spends my money; I am petrified that she'll spend faster than I can earn. Just like my father's habit that landed the whole damn family in Debtors Prison. I feel as if I've been working for centuries: first at the factory, then the attorneys, than as court reporter, now I am compelled to deliver more, yet more, novels. I am a one-man novel-writing factory. I deliver ninety pages a month on average, and I wrote 2,000 pages in a month during <u>Pickwick.</u> The children are voracious, and they all eat and grow beyond their clothes and demand the doctor; but it isn't just the children, it's all the servants I support and my brother Fred and my irresponsible parents. I categorically refuse to assume my father's debts a third time. He's been cutting my signature out of letters and selling them, Mouse says that he "lifts a gold half crown or two every time he visits," [9] and he has of late been forging my name to obtain credit.

(Stops writing.)

Obtain credit. Paint the scene of the counting-house that Mary led you to; see it from the street outside first, like the entrance in the dream. Christmas Eve with a much-too-careful, old man, and the weather will reflect it.

(Writes Carol.)

"Once upon a time – of all good days in the year, on Christmas Eve – old Scrooge sat busy in his counting-house. It was cold, bleak, biting weather . . . The fog came pouring in every chink and keyhole . . . Scrooge had a very small fire, but the clerk's fire was so very much smaller that it looked like one coal . . . Wherefore the clerk . . . tried to warm himself at the candle; in which effort, not being a man of a strong imagination, he failed.

'A merry Christmas, uncle! God save you!' {*Cried a cheerful voice.*} It was the voice of Scrooge's nephew.

'Bah!' {*said Scrooge.*} 'Humbug!'

'Christmas a humbug, uncle!' {*said Scrooge's nephew.*} 'You don't mean that, I am sure.'

'I do,' {*said Scrooge.*} 'Merry Christmas! What right have you to be merry? What reason have you to be merry? You're poor enough.'

'Come, then,' {*returned the nephew gaily.*} 'What right have you to be dismal? . . . You're rich enough.'" [10]

Ha! He's a cheery fool, this flap-mouthed nephew, this over-anxious, face aglow, business failure named Fred, my brother Fred made young.

Act 1, Scene 1

(Charles makes contortions in the mirror. He smiles stupidly as his brother Fred.)

I wonder if this nephew's careful with his funds; certainly my brother Fred is not, he is very much his father's son, whereas I understood very early the import of cash flow. When I was twelve, I divided up my precious earnings into equal piles and wrapped and labeled each one for each day of the week; a hoarded, brown packet a day.
That way I could save up for beer.

"'What's Christmas time to you but a time for paying bills without money; a time for finding yourself a year older, and not an hour richer . . . If I could work my will,' {said Scrooge, *indignantly,*} 'every idiot who goes about with Merry Christmas on his lips, should be boiled with his own pudding, and buried with a stake of holly through his heart . . . Nephew! Keep Christmas in your own way, and let me keep it in mine . . . Much good may it do you! Much good it has ever done you!'

'I have always thought of Christmas time . . . as a good time: a kind, forgiving, charitable, pleasant time: the only time I know of, in the long calendar of the year, when men and women seem by one consent to open their shut-up hearts freely, and to think of people below then as if they really were fellow-passengers to the grave, and not another race of creatures bound on other journeys. And therefore, uncle, though it has never put a scrap of gold or silver in my pocket, I believe that it has done me good, and will do me good; and I say, God bless it!'

The clerk . . . involuntarily applauded." [11]

(Dickens applauds.)

"'Let me hear another sound from you,' {*said Scrooge*}, 'and you'll keep your Christmas by losing your situation.'

'Don't be angry, uncle. Come! Dine with us tomorrow.'

'Why did you get married?' {*asked Scrooge.*}" [12]

(Stops writing.)

"That takes the cake" [13] as my Mouse says. I married my Mouse, and, by marriage to my editor's daughter, I was fulfilling every Englishman's dream of prosperity, of house, home and family. Oh, but, look to this Fred; why did this Fred marry?

(Back to Carol.*)*

"'Because I fell in love.'

'Because you fell in love!' {*growled Scrooge as if that were the only one thing in the world more ridiculous than a merry Christmas!*} 'Good afternoon!'

'Nay, uncle, but you never came to see me before that happened. Why give it as a reason for not coming now?'

'Good afternoon.'

'I want nothing from you; I ask nothing of you; why cannot we be friends?'

'Good afternoon.'

'. . . I have made the trial in homage to Christmas,

Act 1, Scene 1

and I'll keep my Christmas humor to the last. So A Merry Christmas, uncle!'

'Good afternoon.'

'And a Happy New Year!"

'Good afternoon!"' [14]

I like this Scrooge fellow; he's a strong voice and he knows his own opinions, but will he sell books? How can a protagonist who doesn't sanction marriage please my public?

As Charley:
(He's 6 ½. Sound of the door.)

Father, are you done writing your letter to Uncle John Forster?

Charles:
How did you know I was writing a letter to Forster?

As Charley:
You write one almost every day, sir.

Charles:
I don't know what day of the month it is. [15] No, I'm not finished writing.

As Charley:
It's not yet Christmas, sir.

Charles:
What was that?

As Charley:
> You wished me a merry Christmas and it's not Christmas yet. Not for two whole months.

Charles:
> I know the calendar, boy. Tell your mother we might have an impromptu party soon. I have to hear this story aloud. Don't come into the room; don't let any of the pets in here, especially not that mad raven.

(Switching to writing the same letter to Forster.)

Strangely enough, Forster, once again, my characters know each other before I find them. I tell you, despite Thackery's protestations that acting is undignified, I believe my years of amateur acting have aided my writing; I put on the character's oldest shoes and their voices pour from me. Right now, at this moment, some jovial gentleman, some pretentious, old alms-collector, some portly, condescending liberal type aglow with the righteousness of Christmas is stuck in my throat.

(Stops writing the letter and listens.)

"'Scrooge and Marley's, I believe,' {*said one of the gentlemen, referring to his list.*} 'Have I the pleasure of addressing Mr. Scrooge or Mr. Marley?'

'Mr. Marley has been dead these seven years," {*Scrooge replied.*} 'He died seven years ago, this very night.'

... 'At this festive time of the year, Mr. Scrooge,' {*said the gentleman, taking up a pen.*} 'It is more than usually desirable that we should make some slight provision for the poor and destitute.'

... 'Are there no prisons?' {*asked Scrooge*}.

'Plenty of prisons,' {*said the gentleman*}.
... 'And the Union workhouses?' {*demanded Scrooge*}. 'Are they still in operation?'

'They are. Still,' {*returned the gentleman*}. 'I wish I could say they were not.'

'Oh! I was afraid, from what you said at first, that something had occurred to stop them in their useful course,' {*said Scrooge*}. 'I'm very glad to hear it. ... I don't make merry myself at Christmas, and I can't afford to make idle people merry. I help to support the establishments ... mentioned: they cost enough: and those who are badly off must go there.'

'Many can't go there; and many would rather die.'

'If they would rather die,' {*said Scrooge*}, 'they had better do it, and decrease the surplus population.'" [16]

As John Dickens:
(Amplified.)

The sun has set, Charles!

Charles:
You were at fault, father! You bought far too much on credit! Oh, that day, that terrible day when you were arrested for debt, that day I raced in a frenzy from the houses of friend and family alike, through the slippery streets of London, begging for the funds needed to keep you outside prison walls.

As John Dickens:
(Amplified.)

The sun has set on me!

Charles:
Those words from the son of servants who dragged himself up to the level of Navy pay clerk, words "I really believed had broken my heart," [17] they ring in my ears. Stop them, stop them with the story.

(Back to Carol *to banish his father's voice.)*

"'You'll want all day tomorrow, I suppose?' {*Scrooge asked.*}

'If quite convenient, Sir.'

'It's not convenient,' {*said Scrooge*}, 'and it's not fair' . . . 'A poor excuse for picking a man's pocket every twenty-fifth of December!' {*said Scrooge* }. . . 'But I suppose you must have the whole day. Be here all the earlier next morning!' The clerk promised that he would; and Scrooge walked out with a growl.

. . . Scrooge took his melancholy dinner in his usual melancholy tavern and . . . went home to bed. He lived in chambers which had once belonged to his deceased partner . . . Now, it is a fact, there was nothing at all particular about the knocker on the door, except that it was very large.

. . . Let it also be borne in mind that Scrooge had not bestowed one thought on Marley, since his last mention of his seven-years dead partner that afternoon. And then let any man explain to me, if he can, how it happened that Scrooge, having his key in the lock of the door, saw in the knocker . . . not a knocker, but Marley's face . . . It was not angry or ferocious, but looked at Scrooge as Marley used to look . . . The hair was curiously stirred, as if by breath or hot-air; and though the eyes were wide open, they were perfectly motionless . . . As Scrooge looked fixedly at this phenomenon, it was a knocker again. To say that he was not startled . . . would be untrue. But he put his hand upon the key he had relinquished, turned it sturdily, walked in, and lighted his candle." [18]

(Sound of a turning key and opening a door. Sound of banging a door with an echo.)

"Darkness is cheap, and Scrooge liked it . . . He . . . locked himself in; double-locked himself in, which was not his custom. Thus secured against surprise . . . he sat down before the fire to take his gruel." [19]

(Sound of a locking door. Charles eats something off the tray and knocks over the bell on the table.)

"'Humbug!' {*said Scrooge.*} . . . His glance happened to rest upon a bell, a disused bell that hung in the room . . . It was with great astonishment, and with a strange, inexplicable dread, that as he looked, he saw this bell begin to swing. It swung so softly in the outset that it scarcely made a sound; but soon it rang out loudly, and so did every bell in the house." [20]

(Many bell sound cues.)

"This might have lasted half a minute, or a minute, but it seemed an hour. The bells ceased as they had begun, together." [21]

(Bells cease. Sound of clanking chains and the approach of Marley. Sound of cellar door and advancing chains.)

"'It's humbug still!' {*said Scrooge.*} 'I won't believe it.'

His color changed though, when, without a pause, it came on through the heavy door, and passed into the room before his eyes . . . Marley's face! . . . The same face: the very same . . . The chain he drew was clasped about his middle. It was long, and wound about him like a tail; and it was made . . . of cashboxes, keys, padlocks, ledgers, deeds, and heavy purses wrought in steel.

. . . 'How now!' {*said Scrooge, caustic and cold as ever.*} 'What do you want with me?'

As Marley:
(Amplified.)

'Much!'

Charles:
"Marley's voice, no doubt about it.

'Who are you?'

'Ask me who I was.'

'Who were you then?' {*said Scrooge, raising his voice.*} 'In life I was your partner, Jacob Marley . . . You don't believe in me,' {*observed the Ghost.*} . . . 'Why do you doubt your senses?'

'Because,' {*said Scrooge,*} 'a little thing affects them. A slight disorder of the stomach makes them cheats. You may be an undigested bit of beef, a blot of mustard, a crumb of cheese, a fragment of an underdone potato. There's more gravy than of grave about you, whatever you are!'" [22]

(Marley gives a terrible ghost cry – could be actor as Marley and amplified. Sound cue of rattling chains.)

"Scrooge held on tight to his chair, to save himself from falling into a swoon. But how much greater was his horror, when the phantom taking off the bandage round its head, as if it were too warm to wear in-doors, its lower jaw dropped down upon its breast!
Scrooge fell upon his knees, and clasped his hands before his face.

'. . . Why do spirits walk the earth, and why do they come to me?'

'It is required of every man,' {*the Ghost returned*}, 'that the spirit within him should walk abroad among his fellow men, and travel far and wide; and if that spirit goes not forth in life, it is condemned to do so after death . . . and witness what it cannot share, but might have shared on earth, and turned to happiness!'" [23]

(Another terrible ghost cry and rattling chains. Dickens uses one of Mary's scarves as Marley's chain.)

"'I wear the chain I forged in life,' {*replied the Ghost.*} 'I made it link by link, and yard by yard; I girded it on of my own free will, and of my own free will I wore it. Is its pattern strange to you? . . . Or would you know,' {*pursued the Ghost*}, 'the weight and length of the strong coil you bear yourself? It was full and heavy and as long as this, seven Christmas Eves ago. You have labored on it, since. It is a ponderous chain! . . . In life my spirit never roved beyond the narrow limits of our money-changing hole; and weary journeys lie before me!

... 'But you were always a good man of business, Jacob,' *{faltered Scrooge, who now began to apply this to himself.}*

'Business!' *{Cried the Ghost, wringing his hands again.}* 'Mankind was my business. The common welfare was my business; charity, mercy, forbearance, and benevolence, were, all, my business.'

As Marley:
(Amplified.)

'Hear me!'

Charles:
'My time is nearly gone ... I am here tonight to warn you, that you have yet a chance and hope of escaping my fate ... You will be haunted,' *{resumed the Ghost}*, 'by Three Spirits.'

Scrooge's countenance fell almost as low as the Ghost's had done ... 'I think I'd rather not,' *{said Scrooge.}*

'Without their visits,' *{said the Ghost}*, 'you cannot hope to shun the path I tread. Expect the first tomorrow, when the bell tolls one.'

'Couldn't I take 'em all at once, and have it over, Jacob?' *{hinted Scrooge.}*

'Expect the second on the next night at the same hour. The third upon the next night when the last stroke of twelve has ceased to vibrate. Look to see me no more; and look that, for your own sake, you remember what has passed between us!'

... The specter took its wrapper from the table, and bound it round its head, as before ... The apparition walked backward from him; and at every step it took, the window raised itself a little, so that when the specter reached it, it was wide open ... Scrooge ... became sensible of confused noises in the air; incoherent sounds of lamentation and regret; wailings inexpressibly sorrowful and self-accusatory." [24]

(Sound cue of ghosts' wailings.)

"The air was full of phantoms, wandering hither and thither in restless haste and moaning as they went. Every one of them wore chains like Marley's Ghost ... [The] creatures faded into the mist ... and the night became as it had been ... Scrooge closed the window, and examined the door by which the Ghost had entered. It was double-locked ... and the bolts were undisturbed ... And, from the emotion he had undergone, ... or his glimpse of the Invisible World, or the dull conversation with the Ghost, or the lateness of the hour ... [Scrooge] went straight to bed, without undressing, and fell asleep upon the instant." [25]

(Charles collapses into the chair. As he falls asleep.)

Mary? Did you hear all those ghosts? Mary, oh, Mary, why can't I be haunted by you?

(Lights.)

ACT ONE, SCENE TWO
Stave Two: The First of Three Spirits

Charles is still in his study.

Charles:
Remember our first Christmas, Mary? Seven years ago, like the seven years that Marley's been dead, seven years ago when Catherine and I were newly wed and she was so "swollen up" [26] with Charley and you were sixteen and taking care of her and I was writing the end of <u>Pickwick</u> and the beginning of <u>Twist</u>. Catherine was making Charley and I was making Oliver. "I shall never be so happy again as in those chambers three stories high – never if I roll in wealth and fame." [27] You were "the grace and life of our home. We might have known that we were too happy together to be long without a change." [28]

As Catherine:
"She is in a better, far better place, my dear," [29]

Charles:
She said that to me, your big sister, Catherine; I don't know if she believes it. Like you, I was such a sickly child, but my walks invigorate me, Mary. It was a fine walk yesterday out to your grave in Kensal Green, a hearty 10 miles. In the

country, my ears are relieved to be apart from the cacophony of London: the din of children at play, the clatter of servants, drone of street musicians and the barking of dogs. How delightfully clean it is out there, beyond the city's overstuffed and reeking churchyards, the thick smoke, and the filth running in the gutters! Maybe out in the country you would not have gone to your eternal sleep when you were seventeen. Was it only yesterday that I visited you at Kensal Green? It seems so much longer.

"'Why, it isn't possible,' {*said Scrooge,*} 'that I can have slept through a whole day and far into another night? . . . Was it a dream or not?" Scrooge . . . remembered, on a sudden, that the Ghost had warned him of a visitation when the bell tolled one. He resolved to lie awake until the hour was past.

Chimes sound cue:
'Ding, dong!'

Charles:
'A quarter past,' {*said Scrooge, counting.*}

Chimes sound cue:
'Ding, dong!'

Charles:
'Half past!' {*said Scrooge.*}

Chimes sound cue:
'Ding, dong!'

Charles:
'A quarter to it," {*said Scrooge.*}

Chimes sound cue:
'Ding, dong!'

Charles:
'The hour itself,' {*said Scrooge, triumphantly,*} 'and nothing else!' [30]

(Sound of bell sounding one. Flash of light.)

"Lights flashed up in the room upon the instant, and the curtains of his bed were drawn . . . aside, I tell you, by a hand . . . and Scrooge . . . found himself face to face with the unearthly visitor who drew them. . . . It was a strange figure – like a child: yet not so like a child as like an old man, viewed through some supernatural medium, which gave him the appearance of having receded from view, and being diminished to a child's proportions. Its hair, which hung about its neck and down its back, was white as if with age; and yet the face had not a wrinkle in it, and the tenderest bloom was on the skin." [31]

(Dickens uses one of Mary's white nightgowns to portray the ghost.)

"It wore a tunic of purest white; and round its waist was bound a lustrous belt, the sheen of which was beautiful . . . As its belt sparkled and glittered now in one part and now in another, and what was light one instant, at another time dark, so the figure itself fluctuated in its distinctness: being now a thing with one arm, now with one leg, now with twenty legs, now a pair of legs without a head, now a head without a body: of which dissolving parts, no outline would be visible in the dense gloom wherein they melted away.

. . . 'Are you , the Spirit, sir, whose coming was foretold to me?' {*asked Scrooge.*}

As Ghost of Christmas Past:
(Amplified.)

'I am!'

Charles:
. . . 'Who, and what are you?' {*Scrooge demanded.*}

'I am the Ghost of Christmas Past.'

'Long past?'

'No. Your past.'

. . . [Scrooge] then made bold to inquire what business brought him there.

'Your welfare!' {*said the Ghost.*}

Scrooge expressed himself much obliged, but could not help thinking that a night of unbroken rest would have been more conducive to that end. . . . 'Rise! And walk with me!' . . . He rose: but finding that the Spirit made towards the window, clasped its robe in supplication.

'I am mortal,' {*Scrooge remonstrated,*} 'and liable to fall.'

'Bear but a touch of a my hand there,' said the Spirit, laying it upon his heart, 'and you shall be upheld in more than this!'

As the words were spoken, they passed through a wall, and stood upon an open country road,

with fields on either hand. The city had entirely
vanished . . . The darkness and the mist had
vanished with it, for it was a clear, cold winter day,
with snow upon the ground.

'Good heaven!' {*said Scrooge, clasping his hands
together, as he looked about him.*} 'I was bred in
this place. I was a boy here!'" [32]

As a boy in Chatham, I was fairly contented
because I attended school; I loved school. My
sadness came with the horror of surviving
poverty in London! London and Warrens
Blacking and those twenty factory weeks have
tainted everything else around them, like ink
spilled on paper. It was a dark day when the
Dickens family moved to Debtors Prison. I
suffered a kidney attack at the factory, and the
young son of a candle maker graciously offered
to accompany me home. I was too proud to
admit the prison address, and I lied to the candle
maker's son. I heard the lies escape my lips
and watched him believe them. That was my
first lie attached to the prison and the factory,
culminating in my own wife's current ignorance.
That was the school of London streets I attended
in 1824.

"'These are but shadows of the things that
have been,' {*said the Ghost.*} 'They have no
consciousness of us . . . The school is not
deserted,' {*said the Ghost.*} 'A solitary child,
neglected by his friends, is left there still,'

Scrooge said he knew it. And he sobbed.
They approached a mansion of dull red
brick . . . It was a large house, but one of broken
fortunes . . . They went, the Ghost and Scrooge
. . . to a door at the back of the house [into] . . . a

Act 1, Scene 2

long, bare, melancholy room . . . [with] a lonely boy . . . reading near a feeble fire; and Scrooge . . . wept to see his poor forgotten self as he used to be.

. . . [The door] opened; and a little girl, much younger than the boy, came darting in, and putting her arms about his neck, and often kissing him, addressed him as her 'Dear, dear brother. I have come to bring you home, dear brother!

. . . To bring you home, home, home! . . . Father is so much kinder than he used to be, that home's like Heaven! He spoke so gently to me one dear night . . . that I was not afraid to ask him once more if you might come home; and he said Yes, you should . . . And [you] are never to come back here!'

. . . 'Always a delicate creature, whom a breath might have withered,' {*said the Ghost.*} 'But she had a large heart! . . . She died a woman . . . and had, as I think, children.'

'One child,' {*Scrooge returned.*}

'True,' {*said the Ghost.*} 'Your nephew!'

. . . They had but that moment left the school behind them, they were now in the busy thoroughfares of the city . . . The Ghost stopped at a certain warehouse door, and asked Scrooge if he knew it.

'Know it!' {*said Scrooge.*} 'Was I apprenticed here?'

. . . At sight of an old gentleman . . . Scrooge cried {*in great excitement*}: 'Why, it's old

Fezziwig! Bless his heart; it's Fezziwig alive
again!'

Old Fezziwig . . . rubbed his hands; adjusted his
capacious waistcoat; laughed all over himself,
. . . and called out in a comfortable, oily, rich, fat,
jovial voice: 'Yo ho, there! Ebenezer!'

. . . Scrooge's former self, now grown a young
man, came briskly in.

. . . 'Yo ho my boy!" {*said Fezziwig.*} "No more
work tonight. Christmas Eve . . . Clear away, my
lad! And let's have lots of room here! Hilli-ho . . .
chirrup, Ebenezer!'

. . . Every movable was packed off . . . and the
warehouse was snug, and warm, and dry, and
bright a ball-room . . . In came a fiddler." [33]

(Sound of violin music playing waltzes under dance description.)

"In came Mrs. Fezziwig, one vast substantial
smile . . . In came all the young men and women
employed in the business . . . Away they all went,
twenty couples at once, hands half round and
back again the other way; down the middle and
up again; round and round in various stages of
affectionate grouping . . . There was cake . . . and
there was a great piece of cold roast . . . and there
were mince-pies, and plenty of beer." [34]

(Sound of clock striking and music stopped.)

"When the clock struck eleven, this domestic
ball broke up . . . During the whole of this time,
Scrooge had acted like a man out of his wits.
His heart and soul were in the scene, and with
his former self. He corroborated everything,
remembered everything, enjoyed everything, and

underwent the strangest agitation ... He felt the
Spirit's glance, and stopped. 'Nothing particular.
... I should like to be able to say a word or two to
my clerk just now! That's all.'

As Christmas Past:
(Amplified.)

... 'My time grows short.'

Charles:
... This was not addressed to Scrooge, or to
any one whom he could see, but it produced an
immediate effect. For again Scrooge saw himself.
He was older now; a man in the prime of life. His
face had not the harsh and rigid lines of later
years; but it had begun to wear the signs of care
and avarice. There was an eager, greedy, restless
motion in the eye, which showed the passion that
had taken root.

... He was not alone, but sat by the side of a fair
young girl ... in whose eyes were tears, which
sparkled in the light that shone out of the Ghost
of Christmas Past.

... 'Another idol has displaced me ... 'A golden
one.'

'This is the even-handed dealing of the world!'
{*he said.*} 'There is nothing on which it is so
hard as poverty; and there is nothing it professes
to condemn with such severity as the pursuit of
wealth!'
'You fear the world too much ... I have seen your
nobler aspirations fall off one by one, until the
master-passion, Gain, engrosses you.'

... 'What then?' {*he retorted.*} 'Even if I have

grown so much wiser, what then? I am not changed towards you.'

. . . 'Our contract is an old one. It was made when we were both poor and content to be so . . . You are changed.'

. . . 'Have I sought to be released?'

'In words. No. Never.'

'In what, then?'
'In a changed nature; in an altered spirit; in another atmosphere of life; another Hope as its great end. '" [35]

As John Dickens:
(Amplified.)

I'm afraid that selling your books is our only recourse, Charles. The children need milk. Besides, you've read Robinson Crusoe so many times that you must know it by rote.

Charles:
"'Spirit,' {*said Scrooge.*} 'Show me no more! Conduct me home. Why do you delight to torture me?'

As Christmas Past:
(Amplified.)

'One shadow more!'

Charles:
'No more! No more! I don't wish to see it. Show me no more!'" [36]

Show Scrooge the best shadow, the best regret,

his family that would've been, show my tumultuous life, the noisy Eden of a Dickens family Christmas.

"They were in another scene and place: a room, not very large or handsome, but full of comfort. Near to the . . . fire sat a beautiful young girl, so like the last that Scrooge believed it was the same, until he saw her, now a comely matron, sitting opposite her daughter. The noise in this room was perfectly tumultuous, for there were more children there, than Scrooge . . . could count . . . but no one seemed to care; on the contrary, the mother and daughter laughed heartily." [37]

(Sound of door knocking.)

"Such a rush immediately ensued that [the mother] was borne towards it . . . to greet the father, who, came home attended by a man laden with Christmas toys and presents.

. . . And now Scrooge looked on more attentively than ever, when the master of the house, having his daughter leaning fondly on him; . . . and when he thought that such another creature, quite as graceful and as full of promise, might have called him father, and been a spring-time in the haggard winter of his life, his sight grew very dim indeed.

. . . 'Spirit!' {*said Scrooge in a broken voice*}, 'remove me from this place.'

'I told you these were shadows of things that have been,' {*said the Ghost.*} 'that they are what they are, do not blame me!'

. . . 'I cannot bear it! . . . Leave me! Take me back. Haunt me no longer!"

... [Scrooge] was conscious of being exhausted, and overcome by an irresistible drowsiness; and further, of being in his own bedroom ... and had barely time to reel to bed, before he sank into a heavy sleep." [38]

Kensal Green is such a lovely place to sleep; I so want to rest there beside you, Mary, when my time comes, but there's no room for me in the Hogarth family plot. "I cannot bear the thought of being excluded from [your] dust. It seems like losing [you] a second time." [39] You are my comfort and confessor! You are "so much in my thoughts at all times ... that the recollection of [you] is an essential part of my being." [40] You are not a shadow; you are "the dear girl whom I loved, after my wife, more deeply and fervently than anyone on earth." [41] I still wear your ring!

(Pause as he spins the ring around his finger.)

I called for you and instead Scrooge's phantoms haunt me, and I can feel more coming, strange spirits under my skin, pushing up and out through my crooked fingers. *(Dickens slowly takes off Mary's ring and puts it in his vest pocket.)* You are one specter too many. Until this ghost story is finished, Mary, then can I remember you again.

Light down. End of Act One

ACT TWO, SCENE ONE
Stave Three: The Second of Three Spirits
and
Stave Four: The Last of the Spirits

Charles is writing another letter to Forester, recounting a dinner party when he read part of A Christmas Carol *to his family and friends in his Devonshire Terrace house. He is still writing* Carol. *He is not wearing Mary's ring.*

Charles:
Dear Forster, thank you for attending my impromptu dinner party last evening and listening to the first of Christmas Carol's wild spirits. I disagree with your initial reaction. I think a man can find sleep after traveling through his past. I do, though, agree with your grateful appreciation of the blue point oysters served. Directly after dinner, did you hear the comment my wife made to my sister Fanny?

As Catherine:
"If my husband, on occasion, did not let loose and run amuck, as it were, so fulminating are his creative juices, I fear he would burst." [42] But "living in the shadow of Mount Vesuvius one cannot escape unscathed." [43]

Charles:
Mount Vesuvius indeed! I am loathe to admit how well she knows me. If only she didn't talk her

"little nothings" [44] the rest of the day. More later. Scrooge is awaking from my past.

"Awaking in the middle of a prodigiously tough snore . . . Scrooge . . . began to wonder which of his curtains this new specter would draw back, he put them every one aside . . . . for he wished to challenge the Spirit on the moment of its appearance, and did not wish to be taken by surprise and made nervous. . . . Now, being prepared for almost anything, he was not by any means prepared for nothing; and, consequently, when the Bell struck One, and no shape appeared, he was taken with a violent fit of trembling. "[45]

(A bell tolls one.)

"The very core and center of a blaze of ruddy light . . . streamed upon [the bed] when the clock proclaimed the hour; and which being only light, was more alarming than a dozen ghosts . . . He began to think that the source and secret of this ghostly light might be in the adjoining room: from whence, on further tracing it, it seemed to shine.

. . . [He] shuffled in his slippers to the door . . . It was his own room   There was no doubt about that. But it had undergone a surprising transformation. The walls and ceiling were so hung with living green, that it looked a perfect grove, from every part of which, bright gleaming berries glistened . . . Heaped up on the floor, to form a kind of throne, were turkeys, geese, game, poultry . . . great joints of meats, suckling-pigs, long wreaths of sausages, mince-pies, plum-puddings, barrels of oysters . . . and seething bowls of punch, that made the chamber dim with their delicious steam.

Act 2, Scene 1

In easy state upon this couch, there sat a jolly Giant, glorious to see; who bore a glowing torch, in shape not unlike Plenty's horn, and held it up, high up, to shed its light on Scrooge, as he came peeping round the door.

As Christmas Present:
(Amplified.)

... 'Come in! and know me better, man!'" [46]

"'I am the Ghost of Christmas Present,' {*said the Spirit.*} 'Look upon me!'

Charles:
(Dickens can use a cloak as the Present ghost.)

... It was clothed in one simple deep green robe ... bordered with white fur ... Its feet ... were ... bare; and on its head it wore no other covering than a holly wreath set here and there with shining icicles. Its dark brown curls were long and free: free as its genial face, its sparkling eye, its open hand, its cheery voice, its unconstrained demeanor, and its joyful air ... 'You have never seen the likes of me before!' {*exclaimed the Spirit.*}

'Never.... Spirit,' {*said Scrooge submissively,*} 'conduct me where you will. I went forth last night on compulsion, and I learnt a lesson which is working now. Tonight, if you have aught to teach me, let me profit by it.'

'Touch my robe!'

Scrooge did as he was told, and held it fast. Holly, mistletoe, red berries, ivy, turkeys, geese, game, poultry, ... meat, pigs, sausages, oysters, pies, puddings, fruit, and punch, all vanished instantly. So did the room, the fire, the ruddy glow, the hour of night, and they stood in the city streets on Christmas morning.

. . . The Ghost . . . led him straight to Scrooge's clerk's . . . and on the threshold of the door the Spirit smiled, and stopped to bless Bob Cratchit's dwelling with the sprinkling of his torch.

. . . "Then up rose Mrs. Cratchit, Cratchit's wife, dressed out but poorly in a twice-turned gown, but brave in ribbons, which are cheap . . . and she laid the cloth, assisted by Belinda Cratchit . . . also brave in ribbons; while Master Peter Cratchit plunged a fork into the saucepan of potatoes . . . and two smaller Cratchits, boy and girl, came tearing in, screaming that . . . they had smelt the goose, and known it for their own.

'What has ever got your precious father, then?' {*said Mrs. Cratchit.*} 'And your brother Tiny Tim; and Martha warn't as late last Christmas Day!'

. . . In came little Bob, the father, with . . . his thread-bare clothes darned up and brushed, to look seasonable; and Tiny Tim upon his shoulder. Alas for Tiny Tim, he bore a little crutch, and had his limbs supported by an iron frame!

. . . 'And how did Tiny Tim behave?' {*asked Mrs. Cratchit.*}

. . . 'As good as gold,' {*said Bob,*} 'and better. Somehow he gets thoughtful sitting by himself so much, and thinks the strangest things you ever heard. He told me, coming home, that he hoped the people saw him in the church, because he was a cripple, and it might be pleasant to them to remember upon Christmas Day, who made lame beggars walk and blind men see.'

. . . Master Peter and the two ubiquitous young Cratchits went to fetch the goose, with which they soon returned with high procession.

. . . At last the dishes were set on, and the grace was said

. . . 'A Merry Christmas to us all, my dears. God bless us!' Which all the family re-echoed. 'God bless us every one!' Tiny Tim, the last of all.

'Spirit! . . . Tell me if Tiny Tim will live.'

'I see a vacant seat,' {*replied the Ghost,*} 'in the poor chimney corner, and a crutch without an owner, carefully preserved. If these shadows remain unaltered by the Future, the child will die.'

'No, no,' {*said Scrooge.*} 'Oh no, kind Spirit! Say he will be spared.'

. . . 'If he be like to die, he had better do it, and decrease the surplus population.'

Scrooge hung his head to hear his own words quoted by the Spirit, and . . . bent before the Ghost's rebuke, and trembling cast his eyes upon the ground. But he raised them speedily, on hearing his own name.

'Mr. Scrooge!' {*said Bob.*} 'I'll give you Mr. Scrooge, the Founder of the Feast!'

'The Founder of the Feast indeed!' {*cried Mrs. Cratchit, reddening.*} 'I wish I had him here. I'd give him a piece of my mind to feast upon.'
. . . 'My dear,' {*said Bob,*} 'the children; Christmas Day.'

'It should be Christmas Day, I am sure,' {*said she,*} 'on which one drinks the health of such an odious, stingy, hard, unfeeling man as Mr. Scrooge.'

... Scrooge was the Ogre of the family. The mention of his name cast a dark shadow on the party, which was not dispelled for a full five minutes. After it had passed away, they were ten times merrier than before." [47]

(Returning to writing the letter to Forster.)

Forster, what a grand ruckus ensured last evening when we "conjured bravely, that . . . a box of bran changed into a live guinea-pig." [48] Oh, that put some spice in the evening and a bee in Catherine's bonnet!

As Catherine:
We shall have no more guinea pigs in the house this evening, Mr. Forster!

Charles:
It's a wonder she'll let you back into the house. And now Charley wants us to transform his pet raven into a frog.

(Writing <u>Carol</u>.)

"They were not a handsome family. They were not well dressed; their shoes were far from being waterproof; their clothes were scanty; and Peter might have known and very likely did, the inside of a pawnbroker's. But they were happy, grateful, pleased with one another, and contented with the time; and when they faded, they looked happier yet in the bright sprinklings of the Spirit's torch at parting.

Act 2, Scene 1

... It was a great surprise to Scrooge ... to hear a hearty laugh. It was a much greater surprise to Scrooge to recognize it as his own nephew's and to find himself in a bright, dry, gleaming room, with the Spirit standing smiling by his side, and looking at the same nephew with approving affability!

... He said that Christmas was a humbug, as I live!' {*cried Scrooge's nephew.*} '... He's a comical old fellow ... However, his offences carry their own punishment, and I have nothing to say against him ... His wealth is of no use to him. He don't do any good with it. He don't make himself comfortable with it ... I am sorry for him; I couldn't be angry with him if I tried ... He has given us plenty of merriment, I am sure,' {*said Fred,*} ' and it would be ungrateful not to drink to his health ... and I say Uncle Scrooge!'

... 'A Merry Christmas and a happy New Year to the old man, whatever he is!' {*said Scrooge's nephew.*} 'He wouldn't take it from me, but may he have it, nevertheless. Uncle Scrooge!' Uncle Scrooge had imperceptibly become so gay and light of heart, that he would have pledged the unconscious company in return, and thanked them in audible speech, if the Ghost had given him time. But the whole scene passed off in the breath of the last word spoken by his nephew; and he and the Spirit were again on their travels

... It was strange ... that while Scrooge remained unaltered in his outward form, the Ghost grew older, clearly older. Scrooge ... noticed that its hair was gray.
'Are spirits' lives so short?' {*asked Scrooge.*}

As Christmas Present:
(Amplified.)

'My life upon this globe is very brief,' {*replied the Ghost.*}

'It ends tonight.'

Charles:
... 'Tonight at midnight. Hark! The time is drawing near." [49]

(Sound of bells chiming)

'Forgive me if I am not justified in what I ask,' said Scrooge, looking intently at the Spirit's robe, 'but I see something strange, and not belonging to yourself, protruding from your skirts. Is it a foot or a claw!'

... From the foldings of its robe, [the Spirit] brought two children; wretched, abject, frightful, hideous, miserable. They knelt down at its feet, and clung to the outside of its garment ... They were a boy and girl. Yellow, meager, ragged, scowling, wolfish; but prostrate, too, in their humility.

... Scrooge stared back, appalled ... 'Spirit, are they yours?'

... 'They are Man's ... And they cling to me, appealing from their fathers. This boy is Ignorance. This girl is Want. Beware them both, and all of their degree, but most of all beware this boy, for on his brow I see that written which is Doom, unless the writing is erased.'

... 'Have they no refuge or resource?' {*cried Scrooge.*}

Act 2, Scene 1

'Are there no prisons," {*cried the Spirit, turning on him for the last time with his own words.*} 'Are there no workhouses?'" [50]

As John Dickens:
(Amplified.)

Charles will bring in six shillings a week at the warehouse. He has to work; he's run out of books to sell!

Charles:
(Sound of clock chimes.)

"The bell struck twelve. Scrooge looked about him for the Ghost, and saw it not. As the last stroke ceased to vibrate, he remembered the prediction of old Jacob Marley, and lifting up his eyes, beheld a solemn Phantom, draped and hooded, coming, like a mist along the ground, towards him." [51]

(Dickens uses Mary's black bonnet to represent the Ghost of the Future.)

"It was shrouded in a deep black garment, which concealed its head, its face, its form, and left nothing of it, visible save one outstretched hand. But for this it would have been difficult to detach its figure from the night, and separate it from the darkness by which it was surrounded. He felt that it was tall and stately when it came beside him, and that its mysterious presence filled him with a solemn dread.

. . . 'I am in the presence of the Ghost of Christmas Yet to Come?' {*said Scrooge.*}

The Spirit answered not, but pointed downward with its hand.

'You are about to show me shadows of the things that have not happened, but will happen in the time before us,' {*Scrooge pursued.*}

The upper portion of the garment was contracted for an instant in its folds, as if the Spirit inclined its head. That was the only answer he received.

'Ghost of the Future!' {*he exclaimed*}, 'I fear you more than any Spectre I have seen. But, as I know your purpose is to do me good, and as I hope to live to be another man from what I was, I am prepared to bear you company, and do it with a thankful ear. Will you not speak to me?'

It gave him no reply. The hand was pointed straight before them.

'Lead on!'

... The Phantom moved away as it had come towards him. Scrooge followed in the shadow of the dress, which bore him up ..., and carried him along.

They scarcely seemed to enter the city; for the city rather seemed to spring up about them.

... There they were ... amongst the merchants; who hurried up and down, and chinked the money in their pockets ... and looked at their watches ... Scrooge ... looked about in that very place for his own image; but another man stood in his accustomed corner, and ... he saw no likeness of himself among the multitudes ... It gave him little surprise, however; for he had been revolving in his mind a change of life, and thought and hoped he saw his new-born resolutions carried out in this.

Quiet and dark, beside him stood the Phantom, with its out-stretched hand ... They left the busy scene, and went into an obscure part of the town ... The whole quarter reeked with crime, with filth and misery. Far in this den of infamous resort, there was a low-browed, beetling shop ... where iron, old rags, bottles, bones, and greasy offal were bought ... Sitting in among the wares he dealt in ... was a grey-haired rascal ... Scrooge and the Phantom came into the presence of this man, just as a woman with a heavy bundle slunk into the shop.

As Old Woman:
'... Who's the worse for the loss of a few things like these? Not a dead man, I suppose. ... Open that bundle, old Joe, and let me know the value of it. Speak out plain.'

As Old Joe:
'... 'Bed curtains! ... You don't mean to say you took 'em down, rings and all, with him lying there?'

As Old Woman:
'Yes, I do ... Ah! You may look through that shirt till your eyes ache; but you won't find a hole in it, not a threadbare place. It's the best he had, and a fine one too. They'd have wasted it, if it hadn't been for me.'

As Old Joe:
'What do you call wasting of it?' {*asked old Joe.*}

As Old Woman:
> 'Putting it on him to be buried in, to be sure . . . Somebody was fool enough to do it, but I took it off again.'" [52]

Charles:
> "Scrooge listened to this dialogue in horror . . .
>
> 'Spirit!' {said Scrooge, shuddering from head to foot.} 'I see, I see. The care of this unhappy man might be my own. My life tends that way, now. Merciful Heaven, what is this!'
>
> He recoiled in terror, for the scene had changed, and now he almost touched a bed: a bare, un-curtained bed: on which, beneath a ragged sheet, there lay a something covered up, which, though it was dumb, announced itself in awful language
>
> . . . A pale light, rising in the outer air, fell straight upon the bed; and on it, plundered and bereft, unwatched, unwept, uncared for, was the body of this man.
>
> Scrooge glanced towards the Phantom. Its steady hand was pointed to the head. The cover was so carelessly adjusted that the slightest raising of it, the motion of a finger upon Scrooge's part, would have disclosed the face. He thought of it, felt how easy it would be to do, and longed to do it; but had no more power to withdraw the veil than to dismiss the spectre at his side.
>
> . . . 'Spirit! . . . this is a fearful place. In leaving it, I shall not leave its lesson, trust me. Let us go!' Still the Ghost pointed with an unmoved finger to the head.
>
> 'I understand you,' {*Scrooge returned,*} 'and I

would do it, if I could. But I have not the power, Spirit . . . Is there any person . . . who feels emotion caused by this man's death, show that person to me, Spirit! . . . Let me see some tenderness connected with a death.'

The Ghost conducted him through several streets familiar to his feet . . . They entered poor Bob Cratchit's house . . . Quiet. Very quiet. The noisy little Cratchits were as still as statues in one corner . . . The mother and her daughters were engaged in sewing . . . 'It must be near [your father's] time.'

. . . They were very quiet again. At last she said, and in a steady cheerful voice, that only faltered once: 'I have known him [to walk] with Tiny Tim upon his shoulder, very fast indeed . . . But he was very light to carry,' {she resumed, intent upon her work,} 'and his father loved him so, that it was no trouble – no trouble. And there is your father at the door!'

. . . Bob was very cheerful with them, and spoke pleasantly to all the family. He looked at the work upon the table, and praised the industry and speed of Mrs. Cratchit and the girls. They would be done long before Sunday, he said.

'Sunday! You went today, then, Robert?' {*said his wife.*}

'Yes, my dear,' {*returned Bob.*} 'I wish you could have gone. It would have done you good to see how green a place it is. But you'll see it often. I promised him that I would walk there on a Sunday. . . . . I am sure we shall none of us forget poor Tiny Tim.

... 'Specter! ... Tell me what man that was whom we saw lying dead?' The Phantom pointed as before ... A churchyard. Here, then, the wretched man whose name he had now to learn, lay underneath the ground ... Walled in by houses; overrun by grass and weeds, the growth of vegetation's death, not life; choked up with too much burying; fat with repleted appetite ... The Spirit stood among the graves, and pointed down to One.

... 'Before I draw nearer to that stone to which you point,' {*said Scrooge,*} 'answer me one question. Are these the shadows of things that will be, or are they shadows of the things that May be, only? ... Men's courses will foreshadow certain ends, to which, if persevered in, they must lead.

... But if the courses be departed from, the ends will change. Say it is thus with what you show me!'

The Spirit was immoveable as ever.

Scrooge crept towards it, trembling as he went; and following the finger, read upon the stone of the neglected grave his own name.

'Am I that man who lay upon the bed?' {he cried, upon his knees.}

The finger pointed from the grave to him, and back again.

'No, Spirit! Oh, no, no! ... Spirit,' {he cried, tight clutching at its robe,} 'Hear me! I am not the man I was ... Why show me this, if I am past all hope?'

For the first time the hand appeared to shake. . . . 'I will honor Christmas in my heart, and try to keep it all the year. I will live in the Past, the Present and the Future. The Spirits of all Three shall strive within me. I will not shut out the lesson that they teach. Oh, tell me I may sponge away the writing on this stone!'" [53]

I'll visit you, Mary, I promise. I'll bring fresh flowers and keep your stretch of green clear of weeds. I'll not leave you alone! You will not be forgotten!

(Lights out)

ACT TWO, SCENE TWO
Stave Five: The End of It

Charles is reading a letter from Forster in his study.

Charles:
Forster, "I declare I never go into what is called society' that I am not aweary of it, despise it, hate it, and reject it." [54] I make astute observation from a comfortable armchair beside a roaring fire in an elegant house, so I wonder with you if this Scrooge character maintains all his grand, Christmas morning promises for the rest of his life, but, regardless, he's built a protest platform that's stronger than all the combined seats ever offered to me in the House of Commons: social commentary scattered to all levels of a society without unrest and with a reminder of the necessity of order; a reminder to the moneyed class of its social responsibility. I'd rather change the world by writing than by politics, and in the world of Ebenezer Scrooge, order returns with the disappearance of his ghosts.

"Best and happiest of all, the Time before him was his own, to make amends in!

'The Spirits of all three shall strive within me. Oh, Jacob Marley! Heaven, and the Christmas Time

Act 2, Scene 2

be praised for this! I say it on my knees, old Jacob; on my knees!'

He was so fluttered and so glowing with his good intentions, that his broken voice would scarcely answer to his call. He had been sobbing violently in his conflict with the Spirit, and his face was wet with tears.

'They are not torn down!' … "They are here: I am here; the shadows of the things that would have been, may be dispelled. They will be. I know they will! … I don't know what to do!

… I am as light as a feather, I am as happy as an angel, I am as merry as a school-boy. I am as giddy as a drunken man. A merry Christmas to everybody! A happy New Year to all the world. Hallo here! Whoop! Hallo! … It's all right, it's all true, it all happened. Ha, ha, ha! … I don't know what day of the month it is! … I don't know how long I've been among the Spirits. I don't know anything. I'm quite a baby. Never mind. I don't care. I'd rather be a baby. Hallo! Whoop! Hallo here!'" [55]

(Sound of church bells pealing.)

Catherine!

(He rings the bell.)

Charley! Mamie! Catherine!

"Running to the window, he opened it, and put out his head. No fog, no mist; clear, bright, jovial, stirring, cold … Golden sunlight; heavenly sky; sweet fresh air; merry bells. Oh, glorious. Glorious!

[You, there, boy!] 'What's today?'

... 'Today! Why, Christmas Day.'

'It's Christmas Day!' {*said Scrooge to himself.*} 'I haven't missed it. The Spirits have done it all in one night. They can do anything they like. Of course, they can ... Hallo, my fine fellow! ... Do you know the Poulterer's, in the next street but one, at the corner? '

'I should hope I did.'

'An intelligent boy! ... A remarkable boy! Do you know whether they've sold the prize turkey that was hanging up there?'

... 'What, the one as big as me? ... It's hanging there now.'

... 'Go and buy it ... I am in earnest. Go and buy it, and tell 'em to bring it here, that I may give them the direction where to take it. Come back with the man, and I'll give you a shilling. Come back with him in less than five minutes, and I'll give you a half-a-crown!'

The boy was off like a shot.

... 'I'll give it to Bob Cratchit's ... He shan't know who sends it.'

... He dressed himself 'all in his best' and at last got out into the streets. The people were ... pouring forth ... and ... Scrooge regarded everyone with a delighted smile. He looked so irresistibly pleasant, in a word, that three or four good-humored fellows said, 'Good morning, sir! A merry Christmas to you!'

... He had not gone far, when coming on towards him he beheld the portly gentleman, who had walked

into his counting-house the day before and said,
'Scrooge and Marley's, I believe?'

... 'My dear sir, {*said Scrooge,*} quickening his
pace, and taking the old gentleman by both his
hands. 'How do you do? ... A merry Christmas
to you, sir! ... Allow me to ask your pardon.
And will you have the goodness' here Scrooge
whispered in his ear.

'Lord bless me! ... My dear Mr. Scrooge, are you
serious?'

'If you please ... not a farthing less. A great
many back-payments are included in it, I assure
you ... Thank 'ee,' {*said Scrooge.*} 'I am much
obliged to you. I thank you fifty times. Bless you!'

He went to church, and walked about the streets,
and watched people hurrying to and fro, and
patted children on the head." [56]

As Charley:
Father, did you ring?

Charles:
Yes, Charley, I rang and I will in the future
reserve the bell's response for the servants. "I
will live in the past, the present and the future.
The Spirit of all three shall strive within me." [57]
How would you like to go with the entire family to
Italy?

As Charley:
Rome is in Italy, sir.

Charles:
I promise to take you to Rome.

As Charley:
Mamie too? And Kate? And Grip? And baby Walter?

Charles:
All your siblings, but none of the pets. Charley, in my lifetime I have achieved my dreams of a young man: of domestic peace, wealth, literary success, fecundity. The trick is living beyond that. Do you understand?

Charley:
. . . No, sir.

Charles:
I hope you do one day. Meanwhile, find your mother. I wish to speak with her.

"[Scrooge] passed the door a dozen times, before he had the courage to go up and knock. But he made a dash, and did it . . . 'Fred!' Dear heart, alive, how his niece by marriage started!

'Why bless my soul!' {*Cried Fred.*} 'Who's that?'

'It's I. Your Uncle Scrooge. I have come to dinner. Will you let me in, Fred?'

Let him in! It is a mercy he didn't shake his arm off. He was at home in five minutes. Nothing could be heartier . . . Wonderful party, wonderful games, wonderful unanimity, wonderful happiness!" [58]

(Sound of door.)

Mouse, I've decided the family should travel; show the children the world outside England. I'll take a short pause in my writing; I suspect this story might net me a fair amount of profit. I worry too much about money, and I'll try to cease that corroding habit. Money should be carefully spent, if it must, on the children and their education of the world. Will you travel to Italy with me, Mouse?

As Catherine:
Good Heavens, Mr. Dickens, the energy you have. "There is but one Charles Dickens . . . thank God. Two would put me under within a fortnight." [59] Italy! That takes the cake! Well, I'm with you for life, "in for a penny, in for a pound" [60] as they say. Yes, I'll travel where you do as long as we bring the children. I'm worried about you, though, dear, abstaining from all food but oysters and cherries, and I'm rather anxious to mention that "for the past three days [you have] not exhibited any manifestations of [your] amorous nature." [61] Charles, you're not wearing Mary's ring.

Charles:
It's in my pocket. I took it off while I was writing this one. "I often forget in my dreams that I have a dear wife and children; even that I am a man; and wander desolately back to" [62] that terrible time when I was twelve, living alone in a back attic room overlooking a lumberyard. Two springs ago you heard my mother make a "chance remark about some difficult time in [my] early life when [I] was forced to work briefly in the manufacture of the blacking used on boots." [63] This is not one of my mother's imaginings, as you suspected and as I encouraged you to suspect. I worked in Warrens Blacking Warehouse at Hungerford Stairs for twenty weeks. I covered the pots of blacking with paper, ten hours a day, six days a week and at the end of the day I'd walk across Blackfriars Bridge and visit my family in prison.

As Catherine:
. . . I knew about the prison.

Charles:
I resolved to never feel the sting of poverty again; never for my children to know its sharp sting.

As Catherine:
You never shall feel its sting again, dear. You're beyond that now.

Charles:
Forster shall care for the pets in our absence, and I'll ask him to tend to Mary's plot at Kensal Green.

As Catherine:
Charles, did you marry the wrong sister?

Charles:
There was no one else I could've married but you. We never would have had this raucous family otherwise.

As Catherine:
Oh, Charles, gracious, dear, we have the children and this beautiful house and our circle of friends and the world loves your work and you'll write more, so much more. We'll see Italy and Rome and the Coliseum. Whatever shall we pack? Are we traveling over the mountains?

Charles:
(Clock strikes nine and then quarter past.)

"The clock struck nine. No Bob. A quarter past. No Bob. He was full eighteen minutes and a half, behind his time. ... His hat was off, before he opened the door; his comforter too. He was on his stool in a jiffy; driving away with his pen.

'Hallo!' {Growled Scrooge, in his accustomed voice as near as he could feign it.} 'What do you mean by coming here at this time of day?' 'I've very sorry, sir,' {*said Bob.*} 'I am behind my time. . . It's only once a year, sir. . . . It shall not be repeated. I was making rather merry yesterday, sir.'

'Now I tell you what, my friend,' {*said Scrooge,*} 'I am not going to stand this sort of thing any longer. And therefore . . . I am about to raise your salary! . . . A merry Christmas, Bob! . . . A merrier Christmas, Bob, my good fellow, than I have given you, for many a year! I'll raise your salary, and endeavor to assist your struggling family, and will discuss your affairs this very afternoon . . . Make up the fires and buy another coal-scuttle!'

Scrooge was better than his word. He did it all, and infinitely more; and to Tiny Tim, who did NOT die, he was a second father. He became as good a friend, as good a master, and as good a man, as the good old city knew." [64]

(Charles takes Mary's ring out of his pocket.)

Remember, we had been to the theatre that evening, all three of us, and you "went upstairs to bed at about one o'clock in perfect health and [your] usual delightful sprits." [65] I heard the door shut and I heard the cry and the choke and I rushed up. We sent Fred for a doctor. You went in "such a calm and gentle sleep, that although I had held [you] in my arms for some time before. . . . I continued to support [you], long after [you] had fled to Heaven." [66]

(He puts the ring back on his hand.)

Until I see you again, Mary, until I too have moved on to that "undiscovered country, from whose bourn No traveler returns." [67]

(Finishes writing the end of <u>Carol.</u>)

"[Scrooge] had no further [dealings] with the Spirits, but . . . it was always said of him that he knew how to keep Christmas well. . .. . May it truly be said of us, and all of us! And so, as Tiny Tim observed, God Bless Us, Every One!" [68]

(Lights. End of play.)

ENDNOTES

1. *A Christmas Carol*, Charles Dickens
2. *A Christmas Carol*, out of sequence, later in Chapter I
3. *A Christmas Carol*, back in sequence
4. *A Christmas Carol*
5. *A Christmas Carol*
6. Charles Dickens, in a letter to John Forster, February 1840, source is Dickens of London, Wolf Mankowitz
7. Charles Dickens in a letter to John Forster, spring 1838, source is Mankowitz
8. Charles to Catherine Dickens, Cincinnati, April 1842, source is her diary
9. Catherine Dickens about her father-in-law in her diary, March 1842, source is Mankowitz
10. *A Christmas Carol*
11. *A Christmas Carol*
12. *A Christmas Carol*
13. An expression used Catherine Dickens in her diary, March 1842
14. *A Christmas Carol*
15. A *A Christmas Carol*, Scrooge, in the final stave
16. *A Christmas Carol*
17. Charles Dickens' unpublished autobiography, source is Mankowitz
18. *A Christmas Carol*
19. *A Christmas Carol*
20. *A Christmas Carol*
21. *A Christmas Carol*
22. *A Christmas Carol*

23. *A Christmas Carol*
24. *A Christmas Carol*
25. *A Christmas Carol*
26. Catherine Dickens's diary, describing her pregnancy with Walter, April 1842
27. Charles Dickens in a letter at the time of Charles' birth, January 1837, source is Mankowitz
28. Charles Dickens in a letter after Mary's death, 1837, source is Mankowitz
29. Catherine Dickens in her diary, April 1842
30. *A Christmas Carol*
31. *A Christmas Carol*
32. *A Christmas Carol*
33. *A Christmas Carol*
34. *A Christmas Carol*
35. *A Christmas Carol*
36. *A Christmas Carol*
37. *A Christmas Carol*
38. *A Christmas Carol*
39. Charles Dickens, after the Hogarths suffered a double bereavement and needed the plot next to Mary with the death of her brother George in October 1841, source is Mankowitz
40. Charles Dickens, in a letter after Mary's death, source is Mankowitz
41. Charles Dickens, in a letter after Mary's death, source is Mankowitz
42. Catherine Dickens in her diary, February 1842
43. Catherine Dickens in her diary, June 1842
44. Harry Burnett's letter
45. *A Christmas Carol*
46. *A Christmas Carol*
47. *A Christmas Carol*
48. Charles Dickens in a letter to William Charles Macready, 1843, source is Mankowitz
49. *A Christmas Carol*
50. *A Christmas Carol*
51. *A Christmas Carol*
52. *A Christmas Carol*

53. *A Christmas Carol*
54. Charles Dickens in a letter to John Forster, July 1844, source is Mankowitz
55. *A Christmas Carol*
56. *A Christmas Carol*
57. *A Christmas Carol*, out of order
58. *A Christmas Carol*
59. Catherine Dickens' diary, June 1842
60. Expression from Catherine Dickens' diary
61. Catherine Dickens diary, February 1842 "of his active amorous nature. This is unusal except for those times when he is ill."
62. Charles Dickens' unpublished autobiography, source is Mankowitz
63. Catherine Dickens' diary, February 1842
64. *A Christmas Carol*
65. Charles Dickens in letters after Mary's death, source is Mankowitz
66. Charles Dickens in a letter after Mary's death
67. *Hamlet* 3.1, William Shakespeare
68. *A Christmas Carol*

The future of publishing...today!

Apprentice House is the country's only campus-based, student-staffed book publishing company. Directed by professors and industry professionals, it is a nonprofit activity of the Communication Department at Loyola College in Maryland.

Using state-of-the-art technology and an experiential learning model of education, Apprentice House publishes books in untraditional ways. This dual responsibility as publishers and educators creates an unprecedented collaborative environment among faculty and students, while teaching tomorrow's editors, designers, and marketers.

Outside of class, progress on book projects is carried forth by the AH Book Publishing Club, a co-curricular campus organization supported by Loyola College's Office of Student Activities.

Student Project Team for *Dickens of a Carol:*
    Erin Meyer, '08
    Allyson Carroll, '08
    Amanda Reid, '09
    Lauren Fodero, '11

Eclectic and provocative, Apprentice House titles intend to entertain as well as spark dialogue on a variety of topics.

Financial contributions to sustain the press's work are welcomed. Contributions are tax deductible to the fullest extent allowed by the IRS.

To learn more about Apprentice House books or to obtain submission guidelines, please visit www.ApprenticeHouse.com.

Apprentice House
Communication Department
Loyola University Maryland
4501 N. Charles Street
Baltimore, MD 21210
Ph: 410-617-5265
info@apprenticehouse.com

www.ingramcontent.com/pod-product-compliance
Lightning Source LLC
Chambersburg PA
CBHW030005050426
42451CB00006B/116